Learning to Stay

By Joseph Moro

Learning to Stay
© 2026 Joseph Moro
All rights reserved.

Scripture quotations are taken primarily from the NIV, with occasional reference to other translations. Emphasis has been added in places.

This book is not intended to replace professional counseling, pastoral care, or medical advice. If you are experiencing abuse, harm, or feel unsafe, seeking outside help and support is necessary and encouraged.

Learning to Stay is a companion volume to *Stop Running*.

If this book was helpful, reviews help other readers find it.

For my wife Cheri;
who has chosen me again and again, through seasons of closeness and distance, through conversations that were easy and conversations that were hard. This book exists because we stayed.

And for Janis and Michael;
who showed us early on that marriage is not about perfection, but about commitment, humility, and the willingness to keep choosing each other.

And for all those we have learned from,
And for those who trusted us enough to seek our advice along the way;
Your stories, your honesty, and your willingness to wrestle with hard truths gave me the courage to write this book.

Table of Contents

Introduction

Why Staying Is Harder Than Running

Most relationships do not fall apart because people stop loving each other. Love disappears when communication breaks down, and intimacy goes with it.

That breakdown rarely happens all at once. It does not usually begin with betrayal or screaming matches. More often, it starts quietly. Conversations begin to feel heavy. Words are chosen more carefully. Some topics are avoided altogether. Over time, people stop bringing things up, not because they no longer matter, but because they are afraid of what will happen if they do.

Leaving is easy to explain. Staying is not.

Leaving gives you distance and a clear narrative. Staying forces you to sit inside discomfort. It requires you to face misunderstanding, unresolved conflict, and your own reactions when communication fails. Staying demands work that running never asks of you.

This book exists because we did not know how to do that work.

Both Cheri and I grew up in abusive homes. Different kinds of abuse, but the same lesson underneath it. Conflict was unsafe. Emotions were unpredictable. Communication was not modeled. It was endured. We did not enter marriage with the tools we needed. We brought habits shaped by survival, not connection.

We loved each other. That was not the problem.

What we did not know was how to talk when things felt tense. We did not know how to listen without defending. We did not know how to stay engaged when walking away felt easier. So we learned the hard way. Through misunderstandings. Through silence. Through fights where neither of us felt heard. Through moments when it would have been simpler to quit than to figure out how to communicate better.

This book is not written as a clinical or academic text. It is written from lived experience. From mistakes we made. From damage we caused without intending to. From lessons learned slowly, over years, not mastered once and for all.

We are still learning.

This book is also not an argument for staying at any cost. It is not written to convince anyone to remain in an abusive relationship. Abuse requires safety, accountability, and often outside intervention. Sometimes leaving is necessary. Staying is not virtuous if it destroys you. If you are unsure whether what you're experiencing is simply 'unsafe' or truly dangerous, treat that uncertainty itself as a safety question and seek outside help before working harder on communication.

Many relationships are not abusive, but they are unsafe; marked by fear, shutdown, and patterns that make honest communication difficult, not dangerous.

Communication feels tense. Silence feels easier. Conflict feels like a threat instead of a doorway. Over time, intimacy fades not because love is gone, but because it no longer feels safe to talk honestly.

This book is written for those relationships.

Before you read any further, you need to understand how to read this book.

Orientation

What This Book Is

- A practical exploration of how communication breaks down and how it can be repaired

- A guide for learning how to stay engaged when leaving feels easier

- A collection of tools learned over our marriage, not lessons perfected

What This Book Is Not

- A book to help you fix your spouse

- A defense of endurance without change

- A justification for staying in harm

How This Book Works

- You will be asked to judge yourself before you judge your partner

- You will be tempted to read this looking for confirmation that you are right

- The instinct to judge your partner first will limit what you learn

- Discomfort is not a sign this book is wrong. It is often a sign it is honest

If reading this brings awareness of patterns that have existed for years, that awareness is not failure. It is the beginning of repair. Growth does not start when people realize they have done everything right. It starts when they are finally able to see clearly, without defensiveness or despair. This book is not an indictment of past survival. It is an invitation to move forward with intention.

Scripture shapes the mindset this book invites.

> *"Do nothing out of selfish ambition or vain conceit. Rather, in humility value others above yourselves."*
> **Philippians 2:3 (NIV)**

This does not mean erasing yourself or surrendering your voice. It means approaching communication:

- Without the need to win.
- Without the need to defend every reaction.
- Without assuming that being right matters more than being connected.

If you read this book looking to prove that you are already doing everything right, it will not help you. If you read it willing to examine how you listen, how you speak, how you react, and how you protect yourself, it might.

Staying is harder than running because staying requires change.

Not just from your partner.

From you.

That is where this work begins.

Chapter 1

When Conversations Stop Feeling Safe

Most relationships don't explode, they erode.

That breakdown rarely starts with shouting or betrayal. It starts much quieter than that. It begins the first time you hesitate before speaking. The first time you decide something is not worth bringing up. The first time you choose silence because it feels easier than explaining yourself.

At the moment, it feels responsible. Mature. Like you are protecting the relationship.

But that moment matters.

Safety in a relationship is not the absence of conflict. Safety is the belief that honesty will not cost you connection. When that belief weakens, people adapt. They filter what they say. They save conversations for later. They tell themselves timing matters, that they are tired, that this is not the right moment.

Over time, later becomes never.

Cheri and I did not recognize this at first. We thought we were doing well because we were not fighting. What we did not realize was that we were learning how to avoid instead of learning how to talk.

Early in our marriage, our schedules worked against us. We worked opposite shifts. One of us was leaving as the other was coming home. Full days together were rare. Time felt borrowed, short, and fragile.

When time is scarce, conversations change. You talk about what needs to get done. You cover logistics. You handle responsibilities. Deeper conversations get postponed because there never seems to be enough space to handle them well.

At the time, that felt normal. It felt like adulthood. We told ourselves this was just a season, that things would feel different once schedules improved. We were not angry with each other. We were tired. And tired people often mistake silence for peace.

Years later, after starting my career over, we are dealing with opposite shifts and days off again. On the surface, the situation looks the same. The experience does not. Back then, the distance felt like being alone. Now it feels like something that can be named and managed. The difference was never the schedule. It was whether the relationship felt safe enough to hold the strain.

Before we ever had a fight that felt serious, something quieter had already taken root.

We talked less about what we felt and more about what needed to be done. We delayed hard conversations because they felt inconvenient. Exhaustion made honesty feel like extra work. Silence started to feel responsible, even virtuous.

Nothing here felt dramatic. There were no ultimatums. No raised voices. No clear moment where we could say something broke. That is what makes this so dangerous. The relationship was not on fire. It was quietly starving.

Scripture speaks to this posture with uncomfortable clarity.

> *"Everyone should be quick to listen, slow to speak and slow to become angry."*
> **James 1:19 (NIV)**

Listening is not passive. It requires intention. When listening starts to feel unsafe or costly, people stop trying. When people stop trying, distance grows without announcement.

This is why so many couples later say they "grew apart." They did not grow apart. They adapted away from each other. They learned how to function without being fully known. They learned how to coexist without engaging.

At this stage, no one usually feels like the villain. Both people believe they are being reasonable. Both feel misunderstood. Both think the problem is temporary. That is what allows the erosion to continue unnoticed.

If you recognize yourself here, this is not meant to shame you. It is meant to wake you up. Staying requires more than endurance. It requires honesty, even when honesty feels risky.

Before repair is possible, safety has to be restored. Before safety can be restored, it has to be named.

That is where this work begins.

What Was Happening Quietly

- Conversations became shorter and more functional.

- We talked about schedules, tasks, and logistics instead of feelings.

- Hard topics were postponed because timing never felt right.

- Exhaustion made honesty feel like extra work.
- Silence started to feel responsible.

What Safety Was Replaced With

- Honesty was filtered instead of spoken.
- "I'll bring it up later" became a habit.
- Avoidance was mistaken for maturity.
- Keeping the peace mattered more than being understood.
- Speaking felt riskier than staying quiet.

The Cost (Before Anyone Notices)

- Distance grew without a single major fight.
- Intimacy faded without betrayal or crisis.
- Being together began to feel lonely.
- Silence became normal instead of alarming.
- Disconnection looked like stability.

Why This Matters

- Relationships rarely fall apart loudly at first.
- They erode through small, repeated decisions not to speak honestly.

- Safety is not lost all at once. It is traded away slowly.

Questions to Ask Yourself

- Where have I chosen silence instead of honesty to avoid discomfort?

- What conversations have I delayed because they felt risky or inconvenient?

- When I am tired or overwhelmed, what do I stop talking about first?

- Have I mistaken peace for safety?

- Where has silence become normal in my relationship?

Conversation Starters

- "There are things I hold back because I'm not sure how they'll land."

- "I think we avoid some conversations because we're tired, not because they don't matter."

- "What makes conversations feel unsafe for you right now?"

Chapter 2

Listening Beneath the Words

Most relationships don't break because people stop caring. They break because people stop feeling understood.

Misunderstanding does more damage than most people realize. Not because it is dramatic, but because it feels reasonable. Each person believes they are reacting to what the other said. In reality, they are reacting to what they *heard*, filtered through fear, expectation, and past experience.

Cheri and I learned this early in our marriage in a way that stayed with us.

After our wedding, Cheri had borrowed her dress. When it came back from the dry cleaner, it had a stain on it. It looked like someone had set a coffee mug down on the fabric. It was disappointing, but the wedding was over and we moved forward.

Our photographer gave us a physical photo album. This was before digital backups were easy or fast. I decided I wanted to preserve those memories. I carefully removed the photos and began scanning them into the computer one by one at high resolution. It took time and patience. To me, this mattered. I was protecting something important.

Cheri kept asking for the photos. She wanted to give them to her mom.

What I heard was that the work I was doing was unnecessary. That what mattered to me did not matter. I heard criticism.

What Cheri heard was that I did not care about her mom.

Neither of us was trying to hurt the other. Both of us believed we were right. That certainty mattered more to us than understanding.

Her mom only needed one picture. A picture of the dress before it was stained at the end of the reception. We already had it. But she did not explain that at first. And I did not ask.

Instead, I explained myself. I justified what I was doing. I clarified my intent. What I did not do was slow the conversation down and ask why this mattered so much to her.

She stopped explaining because it felt pointless. I kept explaining because I felt misunderstood.

Neither of us felt heard. And once both people feel unseen, conversations stop feeling safe very quickly.

Looking back, the most damaging part of that conflict was not the misunderstanding itself. It was how quickly we both moved into defense. We were no longer listening to understand. We were listening to respond. To protect our position. To prove we were right.

Scripture names the danger in this posture clearly.

> *"To answer before listening, that is folly and shame."*
> **Proverbs 18:13 (NIV)**

Listening stopped the moment certainty took over.

What Actually Happened

- I assumed I already knew why she wanted the photos.

- She assumed I had already decided her concern did not matter.

- I explained instead of asking.

- She stopped explaining because it felt unsafe to keep trying.

- We both defended our position instead of protecting the relationship.

The Problem Beneath the Problem

- Certainty replaced curiosity.

- Listening became a way to prepare a response.

- Understanding felt like losing.

- The goal shifted from connection to winning.

Defensive certainty is destructive.

Once both people decide they are right, listening stops. Conversations stop being about understanding and become about proving a point. Safety disappears long before the argument ends.

The Cost (Often Missed)

- I got louder.

- She got quieter.

- The conversation ended without resolution.

- What looked like peace was actually withdrawal.

One person winning does not make a relationship safer.

One person going quiet does not make a relationship healthier.

Silence can hide damage just as easily as shouting.

Key Points

- What you hear is shaped by fear and assumption.
- Explaining intent does not restore safety.
- Defensiveness shuts down listening.
- Silence is not the same as resolution.
- Defensive certainty destroys connection.

Questions to Ask Yourself

- When I feel misunderstood, do I try to understand or try to win?
- How quickly do I move into defense during conflict?
- Have I mistaken my spouse going quiet for agreement or peace?
- Where has certainty replaced curiosity in my conversations?
- What does my spouse do when conversations stop feeling safe?

Conversation Starters

- "This is what I heard, and this is how it made me feel. Can you help me understand what you meant?"

- "I think I'm defending my position instead of listening right now."

- "Did you stop talking because it felt unsafe to keep going?"

Next we'll look at listening beneath the words…

Chapter 3

Two Sides of the Same Conflict

How to Read the Next Two Chapters

The next two chapters are written differently than the rest of this book.

They are not meant to be read in order.

They are meant to be read **starting with yourself**.

Most conflict between couples is not caused by one person being right and the other being wrong. It is caused by two people responding differently when tension rises. One pushes to talk and resolve. The other pulls back to process and calm down. Both believe they are protecting the relationship. Both often end up making things worse.

Before you read further, you need to decide which response is more natural for you **when conflict is present**.

If you are someone who tends to push toward conversation, resolution, or fixing when something feels wrong, start with **Chapter 3A**.

You may recognize yourself if:

- Silence makes you anxious

- You want to talk things through immediately

- Distance feels like rejection

- You explain yourself quickly when misunderstood

- You believe resolving conflict quickly shows commitment

- You get louder or more insistent when you feel unheard.

If you are someone who tends to need space, quiet, or time to process before talking, start with **Chapter 3B**.

You may recognize yourself if:

- You need time alone to calm down before speaking

- Talking too soon feels overwhelming

- You shut down when conversations escalate

- You let small things go to avoid conflict

- You internalize rather than push back

- You feel pressured when asked to talk immediately

If you see yourself in **both lists**, do not get stuck on labels.

Most people are not one thing all the time. Think about what you default to **first** when tension rises. Start there.

Read the chapter that confronts your instinct **before** reading the one that explains your partner.

That order matters.

Understanding your spouse without understanding yourself will only reinforce defensiveness. These chapters are meant to remove excuses, not provide them.

Once you finish the section written for you, you will be directed to read the other half. Do not skip it. You cannot understand how conflict works in your relationship by examining only one side of it.

These two chapters describe patterns, not identities. They explain how people react under stress, not who they are at their best.

What you recognize here is not meant to shame you. It is meant to make you honest.

Only after both sides are understood can repair begin.

Chapter 3A

When You Need to Fix It Now

(Fixer)

If you are someone who feels a strong pull to talk, fix, or resolve conflict immediately, this chapter is written for you.

When something feels wrong, you feel it in your body. Silence feels dangerous. Distance feels like rejection. Waiting feels irresponsible. You want clarity, reassurance, and resolution. You want to know where things stand.

To you, talking it through right away feels like caring.

That instinct is not wrong. But it is often misunderstood.

Early in our marriage, this was me.

When tension showed up, I wanted to address it immediately. I believed that if we could just talk it out, things would settle. I equated urgency with commitment. The faster we resolved it, the safer the relationship would be.

What I did not understand was how that urgency landed on the other side.

When I pushed to talk, Cheri did not feel cared for. She felt pressured. When I followed her to continue the conversation, she did not feel pursued. She felt cornered. My need to fix felt to her like a demand to perform emotionally before she was ready.

I was trying to restore connection. She was trying to protect herself.

From my perspective, silence felt like abandonment. From hers, my urgency felt like escalation.

So I pushed harder.

I explained myself. I repeated my point. I raised my voice, not because I wanted to intimidate, but because I wanted to be heard. What I didn't see was that the louder I got, the less safe the conversation became.

At some point, the issue we were arguing about stopped mattering. The conversation became about my need for answers versus her need for space. I believed I was fighting for the relationship. In reality, I was fighting my own anxiety.

Fixers often confuse resolution with safety. If the problem is named, discussed, and settled, then everything is okay. But forcing resolution too soon does not create safety. It replaces it with compliance.

This is where fixers can do real damage without realizing it.

When you push for answers before your partner is ready, you are asking them to prioritize your discomfort over their capacity. When you insist on talking now, you may be teaching them that their emotions are only acceptable on your timeline. By capacity, I do not mean willingness or capability. I mean the emotional and mental space a person has available to engage safely in that moment.

Over time, many processors learn a painful lesson. It is easier to go quiet than to engage. It is easier to let small things go than to risk escalation. The argument ends. The room gets calm. You feel relieved.

But the cost has simply shifted.

Scripture warns against this kind of unchecked urgency.

> *"Fools give full vent to their rage, but the wise bring calm in the end."*
> **Proverbs 29:11 (NIV)**

This is not about anger alone. It is about restraint. Wisdom knows when speaking is helpful and when it is harmful. Wanting to talk is not the same as being ready to listen.

If you are a fixer, your urgency may come from care, fear, or both. But intent does not cancel impact. When your partner feels pressured, they do not feel safe. When they do not feel safe, they cannot communicate honestly.

That is the opposite of what you want.

Fixers often believe that silence means the problem is getting worse. Sometimes it is. But sometimes silence is the only thing preventing further damage in the moment. When you ignore that, you may be training your partner to disappear emotionally rather than stay engaged.

That is not connection. That is control.

This does not mean you should suppress your need to talk or pretend issues do not matter. It means you need to understand what your urgency costs the person on the other side.

Before you decide what your partner should do differently, you need to understand how your behavior lands when emotions are already high.

What This Pattern Looks Like

- You push for conversation as soon as tension appears.

- You repeat your point when you feel misunderstood.

- You equate space with avoidance.

- You feel dismissed when your partner needs time.

- You get louder or more insistent under stress.

The Cost You May Not See

- Your partner feels pressured instead of heard.

- Conversations feel unsafe before they even begin.

- Silence becomes a coping mechanism.

- Compliance replaces honesty.

- Intimacy erodes quietly.

Questions to Ask Yourself

- When I push to talk immediately, what am I actually afraid of?

- Do I listen to understand, or listen to respond?

- How do I react when my partner asks for space?

- Have I mistaken urgency for care?

- What might my partner be protecting themselves from when they step away?

If you are a fixer, this chapter is not meant to shame you. It is meant to slow you down.

Understanding your own instinct is necessary, but it is not enough.

Now read **Chapter 3B**.

You need to understand what silence feels like from the inside, just as you want your need to talk to be understood.

Only then can you begin to see the full pattern at work.

Chapter 3B

When Silence Feels Safer Than Speaking

(Processor)

If you are someone who needs space, quiet, or time to process before talking, this chapter is written for you.

When emotions rise, your first instinct is not to engage. You need room to breathe. Time to think. Space to sort through what you are feeling before you can speak honestly. Talking too soon feels overwhelming. Words come out wrong. The risk of escalation feels real.

That instinct is not wrong. But it can still cause damage.

Early in our marriage, this was often Cheri.

When conversations became intense, she needed to step away. She needed time alone to calm down and figure out what she wanted to say. Staying in the conversation felt unsafe. Leaving it felt like self-protection.

From her perspective, space prevented harm.

From mine, it felt like abandonment.

When Cheri went quiet, I did not experience it as patience or wisdom. I experienced it as withdrawal. The longer the silence lasted, the louder my anxiety became. I filled the gap with assumptions. I believed she was avoiding the issue, refusing to engage, or unwilling to admit fault.

So I pushed.

And the more I pushed, the less safe it felt for her to return.

Processors often believe that silence prevents damage. Sometimes it does. But silence can also delay it. When space becomes the only way to survive conflict, it stops being a pause and becomes a pattern.

This is where processors can do real harm without realizing it.

When you step away without naming your intention to return, you leave your partner alone with the tension. When you let small things go repeatedly to avoid conflict, you teach the relationship that your voice is optional. The conversation may end, but the issue does not.

Over time, many processors internalize their hurt. They convince themselves it is not worth bringing up. They tell themselves they are being mature. They choose calm over honesty.

The room stays quiet.
The distance grows.

In some arguments, processors will try to fix first. They engage, push, and attempt resolution. When that effort fails or becomes overwhelming, they retreat even further. To the other person, this feels confusing. The shift from engagement to silence feels like rejection, not regulation.

What is actually happening is capacity being exceeded.

Scripture speaks to the danger of withholding truth.

"An honest answer is like a kiss on the lips."
Proverbs 24:26 (NIV)

Honesty here does not mean immediacy. It means presence. Silence that never returns is not wisdom. It is absence.

Processors often believe that letting things go keeps the peace. What it often keeps is imbalance. One person speaks. The other absorbs. One person feels heard. The other feels invisible.

That is not safety. That is self-erasure.

Needing space does not mean you get to disappear from the conversation entirely. Processing is not an excuse to avoid. Silence is not a substitute for resolution.

If you are a processor, your instinct may come from a desire to prevent harm. But when silence becomes your primary response, it teaches your partner that connection is conditional. That honesty must wait. That your inner world is closed off.

That is not the message you want to send.

What This Pattern Looks Like

- You step away when emotions rise.

- You need time alone to think before speaking.

- You shut down when conversations escalate.

- You let small things go to avoid conflict.

- You internalize hurt instead of naming it.

The Cost You May Not See

- Your partner feels abandoned instead of respected.

- Anxiety grows in the absence of communication.

- Important issues remain unresolved.

- Resentment builds quietly.

- Intimacy fades without obvious conflict.

Questions to Ask Yourself

- When I go quiet, do I clearly communicate my intention to return?

- Have I confused peace with safety?

- What do I avoid saying because it feels risky?

- How might my silence be landing on my partner?

- What has it cost me to keep things to myself?

If you are a processor, this chapter was written for you.

Now read **Chapter 3A**.

Understanding yourself is not enough. You also need to understand what your silence costs the person who is waiting for you to come back.

Only after both sides are understood can the pattern be named honestly.

Chapter 3C

When different responses Collide

Up to this point, I've described patterns that show up repeatedly in our marriage. One of us tends to fix. One of us tends to process. That framing matters because it explains why our conflicts followed predictable paths for years.

But it was never meant to lock us into permanent roles.

Stress has a way of changing what we need from each other. When life presses hard enough, the person who usually fixes may need space. The person who usually processes may need to speak. These patterns are not identities. They are responses. And every marriage will encounter moments when those responses shift.

That's why learning these patterns matters even if you don't fit neatly into one side all the time.

Different combinations of responses can all work. None of them work automatically.

Two fixers can make a relationship function. Problems get addressed quickly. Conversations happen fast. The danger is escalation. When both people push at the same time, listening often disappears. Volume replaces understanding. Resolution may come, but it is often shallow. The conflict ends before either person feels fully heard.

Two processors can also make a relationship work. Calm is preserved. Space is respected. Emotions are handled carefully. The danger here is delay. When both people wait for the right moment, the moment may never come. Important issues stay buried. Peace becomes a substitute for honesty.

When one person fixes and the other processes, conflict often feels personal. One partner feels abandoned. The other feels pressured. Timing becomes the battleground instead of the issue itself. Both believe they are protecting the relationship. Both feel misunderstood.

That combination describes most of our marriage.

I default toward fixing. Cheri defaults toward processing. When tension rose, I wanted to talk. She needed space. When she stepped away, I pushed harder. When I pushed harder, she withdrew further. The pattern fed itself, and for a long time we didn't know how to interrupt it.

But the pattern was not fixed.

After decades in one career, I changed jobs. It wasn't just a professional shift. It affected our schedule, our finances, and how secure I felt in my role as a husband and father. For the first time in a long while, I wasn't trying to fix anything immediately. I needed time. I needed space to process what the change meant for our family and for me.

When I came back to those conversations, what I needed wasn't solutions. I needed reassurance. I needed emotional support. I needed to know I wasn't failing the people I loved.

In those moments, the roles reversed.

Cheri was steady. She spoke. She stayed present. She offered support instead of space. And I was the one who needed time before I could talk clearly.

The pattern changed, but the principles didn't.

Most people aren't one thing all the time. They have a primary response under stress and often a secondary one that appears when pressure increases. Under moderate stress, the default shows up. Under heavier stress, the secondary response takes over. When both fail, people either shut down completely or escalate sharply.

That switching isn't manipulation. It's overload.

The real damage happens when these responses collide without being understood. When urgency is interpreted as control. When silence is interpreted as punishment. When both people assume the worst instead of recognizing stress responses at work.

Understanding this doesn't excuse harm. It increases responsibility.

Once you can name the pattern, you stop reacting blindly. You begin to understand why the same arguments repeat, why timing feels impossible, and why both of you can walk away feeling unheard even when neither of you intended harm.

I'm not explaining this so you can label your marriage. I'm explaining it so you can stop being confused by it.

When you notice your partner switching responses mid-conflict, it usually means something important has changed. The conversation has crossed from uncomfortable into overwhelming. What worked a few minutes ago no longer does.

That shift isn't a tactic. It's a signal. And if it goes unnoticed or is misread, conflict escalates quickly.

Key Points

- Fixing can look like control when it is driven by fear.

- Processing can look like avoidance when capacity is exceeded.

- Switching responses usually means stress has surpassed what the default can handle.

- Urgency can create connection or escalate conflict depending on whether it listens.

- Silence can protect or damage depending on whether it returns.

- Conflict becomes destructive when neither response is named or understood.

Different responses do not doom a relationship. Unexamined responses do.

In the next chapter, we will talk about what repair actually looks like when neither person is wrong, but both have been hurt.

Chapter 4

How Repair Starts

Repair is not the moment everything feels better.

Repair is the moment two people decide to return to a conversation that already hurt.

Most couples believe repair happens when an argument ends. When voices lower. When time passes. When things feel calmer. What usually happens instead is avoidance. Silence gets mistaken for peace. Distance gets mistaken for healing.

Conflict will happen again. That is not a failure of communication. It is part of being in a relationship between two imperfect people. What determines whether a marriage grows or erodes is not whether conflict happens, but whether there is a way back when it does.

- Repair does not erase damage.
- Repair does not guarantee agreement.
- Repair does not prevent future conflict.
- Repair starts with a choice to return.

What We Mean by Repair

Before going any further, it matters to be clear about what repair actually is.

Repair starts when defensiveness stops.
Repair starts with acknowledging impact, not intent.
Repair does not require agreement.
Repair does not require the conversation to finish.
Repair keeps the relationship open for what comes next.

That's it.

If repair feels difficult, it's because it is. Returning to a conversation where someone was hurt requires humility. It requires setting aside the need to be right long enough to understand what happened.

Most couples never get here.

Why Repair Rarely Happens

Repair is avoided for understandable reasons.

Time feels easier than reopening pain. Silence feels safer than risking another argument. Apologies get rushed because discomfort is high. Explanations are offered because being misunderstood feels unbearable.

But explanations do not repair damage.

Saying "that's not what I meant" may be true, but it often deepens the wound. Being misunderstood hurts, even when intentions were good. Explaining intent centers your experience when the other person is still dealing with impact.

This is where many conversations stall permanently.

Fixers explain because they want clarity and safety.
Processors stay silent because they want calm and control.

Both believe they are protecting the relationship. Both can unintentionally make repair harder.

Explanation Is Not Repair

This distinction matters more than most people realize.

Explanation focuses on intent.
Repair focuses on impact.

Explanation sounds like:

- "That's not what I meant."

- "You took it the wrong way."

- "I was just trying to help."

Repair sounds different because it is different.

Repair does not argue with how something landed. It starts by acknowledging that it did.

This is why one of the most effective ways to re-enter a damaged conversation begins with a simple posture shift:

This is what I heard, and this is how it made me feel.

That statement does not assign blame.

It does not demand agreement.

It does not accuse intent.

It creates space.

It says: *something landed here, even if that wasn't what you meant.*

Repair cannot happen until that landing is acknowledged.

Timing the Return

Repair also depends on timing, not because timing fixes everything, but because mistimed repair can reopen wounds instead of healing them.

Repair attempted too soon can feel unsafe.

Repair delayed too long can feel dismissive.

Willingness matters more than speed.

One of the most important things we learned in our marriage was how to return without restarting the fight. That meant learning to ask whether the other person was ready instead of demanding resolution. It meant accepting "not yet" without interpreting it as refusal. It meant expressing calm availability without pressure.

Repair often starts with something as simple as:

- "I'm ready to talk when you are."

- "I want to understand what happened."

- "I don't need to solve this right now."

Those statements don't fix the issue.
They reopen the door.

What Repair Is Not

Repair is not giving in.

Repair is not minimizing hurt.

Repair is not erasing boundaries.

Repair is not tolerating abuse.

Repair is not staying silent to keep peace.

If a relationship is unsafe, repair is not the goal. Protection is. Nothing in this chapter is meant to convince someone to remain in a harmful or abusive situation.

Repair is about restoring honesty and safety where both people are willing to return.

Why Repair Matters Before Staying

Repair does not mean everything is fixed.

It means the relationship is still open.

When repair starts, the conversation can return without one person needing to win and the other needing to disappear. Safety is reestablished enough for honesty to exist again. That matters, but it is not the end of the work.

Repair opens the door. What happens after that determines whether the relationship actually grows.

Staying is not proven by how well you handle conflict in the moment. It is proven by what you are willing to value afterward. Whether you make room for what matters to the other person. Whether their needs, interests, and callings are treated as essential or optional. Whether partnership outweighs convenience.

Repair makes staying possible.

Willingness is what makes staying real.

In the next chapter, we'll talk about what that willingness looks like in practice. Not agreement. Not sameness. Not control. But buying into what matters to the other person, even when it doesn't naturally matter to you.

That is what keeps connection from quietly eroding over time.

Chapter 5

Buying Each Other's Chairs

Support in a relationship isn't proven in agreement. It's proven in willingness.

One of the quiet ways connection erodes is when what matters to one person consistently feels optional to the other. Not dismissed outright, just postponed, minimized, or treated as less important than practicality or efficiency.

Over time, that sends a message: this part of you doesn't really fit here.

Buying each other's chairs is about reversing that message.

Buying each other's chairs isn't about money. It's about buying into what matters to the other person, even when it doesn't naturally matter to you.

The phrase comes from the idea that when you care about someone, you do more than tolerate what matters to them. You invest in it. You buy into it. In a shared life, that means recognizing that what grounds one person may look very different from what grounds the other, and choosing to support it anyway.

Every person has things that ground them. Interests, routines, spaces, callings, or passions that help them feel like themselves. Marriage doesn't erase those needs, but it often pressures them into the background. Responsibilities pile up. Efficiency takes over. What once felt important gets labeled unnecessary or inconvenient.

In our marriage, buying each other's chairs has looked very practical.

Cheri has bought mine by making room for things that ground me, even when they weren't convenient. Woodworking takes space. Tools take space. Time at a computer takes space. None of those things are efficient when you're raising kids or managing a household. But instead of treating them as distractions, she treated them as necessary. She made room for them, not once, but repeatedly, in different seasons.

I've bought Cheri's chairs the same way. In every place we've lived, there has been an art room. Not because it was always the easiest use of space, but because creating is part of who she is. It wasn't optional. It wasn't something to be justified or delayed until life slowed down. It mattered, so we made room.

Those decisions didn't solve problems or eliminate stress. They communicated something more important: what matters to you matters here. Not conditionally. Not temporarily. As part of the life we're building together.

Support says something very specific.

- I see that this matters to you

- You don't need to justify it

- I'm willing to make room

Scripture returns to this posture again.

"Do nothing out of selfish ambition or vain conceit. Rather, in humility value others above yourselves."
Philippians 2:3 (NIV)

Valuing someone includes valuing what gives them life.

Support is often misunderstood because people assume it requires agreement. It doesn't.

You don't have to share your spouse's interests to support them. You don't have to fully understand a passion to respect it. Support is not enthusiasm. Support is permission.

- Permission to care

- Permission to invest time

- Permission to take up space

Many conflicts aren't actually about disagreement. They're about legitimacy. When one person constantly has to explain or defend why something matters, the relationship becomes conditional.

Scripture reminds us that love is demonstrated, not declared.

> *"Let us not love with words or speech but with actions and in truth."*
> **1 John 3:18 (NIV)**

Sometimes love looks like encouragement. Sometimes it looks like stepping aside.

One of the clearest ways support is felt is through space. Physical, emotional, or relational.

When someone is given room to pursue what matters to them, they feel trusted. When space is consistently questioned or delayed, they feel constrained. This isn't unlimited freedom without consideration. It's intentional accommodation.

Scripture affirms rest and renewal.

"Come with me by yourselves to a quiet place and get some rest."
Mark 6:31 (NIV)

Rest includes mental and creative space, not just physical recovery.

Support begins to fail when it becomes conditional.

Conditional support sounds like:

- "That's fine, but only if…"

- "We can do that later."

- "Is that really necessary?"

- "That doesn't make sense to me."

Over time, conditional support trains people to shrink their needs rather than share them. They learn which parts of themselves are welcome and which are tolerated.

Scripture warns against this posture.

"Each of you should look not only to your own interests, but also to the interests of others."
Philippians 2:4 (NIV)

Looking to another's interests requires intention.

When support is withheld, control often takes its place.

- Control questions motives

- Control monitors choices

- Control requires justification

Partnership assumes goodwill.

Scripture contrasts these approaches clearly.

"You were called to be free... rather, serve one another humbly in love."
Galatians 5:13 (NIV)

Freedom and service coexist when love leads.

Buying each other's chairs is mutual. It's not one person sacrificing while the other thrives. It's both people being supported in becoming their best selves. Over time, this kind of partnership builds trust, openness, and willingness to engage.

Scripture reminds us why this matters.

"Two are better than one, because they have a good return for their labor."
Ecclesiastes 4:9 (NIV)

Support multiplies strength.

Staying well isn't about sameness. It's about making room.

Key Points

- Support is proven by willingness, not agreement

- Valuing your partner includes valuing what matters to them

- Support does not require understanding, only respect

- Conditional support trains people to shrink themselves

- Control replaces partnership when support is withheld

- Mutual investment strengthens long-term connection

Questions to Ask Yourself

- What matters deeply to my spouse that I tend to minimize or postpone?

- Where have I required agreement before offering support?

- What parts of my partner feel optional to me right now?

- Where has efficiency mattered more than connection?

- What would it look like to make room instead of asking for justification?

Chapter 6

Control vs. Unity

Every relationship eventually chooses between control and unity.

Control prioritizes predictability.

Unity prioritizes trust.

Control manages behavior.

Unity protects connection.

Most couples do not consciously choose control. They drift there. Fear goes unnamed. Uncertainty feels dangerous. Support begins to feel risky. And slowly, what once looked like partnership turns into management.

Fear is usually what pushes relationships toward control, even when people believe they are being reasonable.

How Fear Pulls Relationships Toward Control

Fear rarely announces itself as fear.

It sounds like logic.

It sounds like responsibility.

It sounds like concern.

Fear says things like:

- "That doesn't make sense."
- "That's not practical."
- "Let's be realistic."
- "We need to be careful."

Those statements aren't always wrong. But when fear becomes the deciding factor, unity begins to erode.

Fear wants certainty. Unity requires trust.

When fear is left unnamed, it looks for structure. That structure often becomes control.

Control Is Not Safety

One of the most common mistakes in marriage is believing that control creates safety.

It doesn't.

Control creates compliance, not connection. It produces short-term stability at the cost of long-term intimacy. People adapt. They shrink. They stop bringing forward the parts of themselves that feel inconvenient or risky.

Over time, the relationship becomes orderly and empty.

Control manages outcomes.

Unity shares risk.

Scripture speaks clearly to this tension.

"Fear of man will prove to be a snare."
Proverbs 29:25 (NIV)

Freedom and love can coexist. Control and unity cannot.

How Control Quietly Replaces Support

Control almost never begins as domination. It begins as management.

- Management of time
- Management of priorities
- Management of energy
- Management of expectations

At first, it feels helpful. Responsible. Even loving. But when one person's fear starts shaping what is allowed, delayed, or dismissed, partnership shifts.

Control questions motives instead of trusting intent.

Control requires justification instead of listening.

Control prioritizes efficiency over connection.

Support becomes conditional. Unity becomes fragile.

Control vs Unity in Practice

Control sounds like:

- "That's fine, but only if…"

- "Let's revisit that later."

- "Why do you need that?"

- "That doesn't seem necessary."

Unity sounds different:

- "I don't fully understand, but I see it matters to you."

- "Let's make room for that."

- "I trust you with this."

- "We'll figure it out together."

Unity does not eliminate fear. It refuses to let fear dictate the terms of the relationship.

Naming Fear Restores Choice

The goal is not to eliminate fear. Fear is human.

The goal is to name it before it hardens into control.

Unnamed fear creates rules.

Named fear creates conversation.

Fear sounds different when it is owned:

- "I'm afraid of losing stability."

- "I'm afraid this will cost us more than we can afford."

- "I'm afraid I won't be enough if this changes."

Naming fear restores choice. Control removes it.

Scripture reminds us what fear does when left unchecked.

> *"For God has not given us a spirit of fear, but of power, love, and self-discipline."*
> **2 Timothy 1:7 (NIV)**

Fear narrows. Love expands.

Unity Requires Courage

Unity costs more than control.

Control feels efficient.

Unity feels risky.

Unity requires believing your partner's growth is not a threat to your stability. It requires choosing trust over management. It requires making room even when outcomes are uncertain.

This is where many relationships stall. Control feels safer. Unity feels vulnerable.

But unity is where connection survives.

Key Points

- Every relationship moves toward either control or unity

- Fear is the primary driver of control

- Control produces compliance, not intimacy

- Unity prioritizes trust over predictability

- Unnamed fear reshapes relationships silently

- Naming fear restores partnership and choice

Questions to Ask Yourself

- Where have I used control to manage fear instead of naming it?

- What am I trying to make predictable instead of trusting my partner with?

- Where has support become conditional in my relationship?

- What fear do I avoid naming because it feels unsafe or vulnerable?

- What would choosing unity over control require of me right now?

Chapter 7

When Exhaustion Replaces Engagement

Most marriages don't end in explosions.

They end in exhaustion.

Not anger.

Not hatred.

Not even constant conflict.

Just tiredness.

People stop pushing. Stop asking. Stop bringing things up because it feels easier to let them go than to fight again. Conversations become logistical. Time together becomes functional. What once felt connected starts to feel distant, but manageable.

And that's the danger.

When Numbness Feels Like Peace

There was a point in our marriage where we talked about divorce.

Not casually. Not hypothetically. It came after a real fight. Yelling. Raised voices. Emotional exhaustion.

I don't remember what the argument was actually about. That part didn't matter.

What mattered was what came after.

The fight itself was over something small. Something stupid. But it wasn't really about that. It was the release of months of burnout, numbness, and unspoken frustration. We weren't buying each other's chairs the way we needed to. We weren't making room for time together. We weren't having the conversations we kept postponing because they felt uncomfortable or inconvenient.

The relationship hadn't exploded. It had worn down.

That's how most people get there.

Numbness can feel like peace if you're tired enough. Less conflict feels like improvement when you don't have the energy to engage. But silence is not resolution. It's postponement.

The Quiet Signs of Disengagement

Exhaustion changes how people show up long before it changes whether they stay.

Here's what that erosion often looks like:

- Conversations become purely functional

- Time together feels rare or rushed

- Difficult topics stay avoided "for now"

- Needs shrink instead of being shared

- Conflict feels pointless instead of necessary

People don't stop caring. They stop believing engagement will help.

That's the shift.

When Divorce Gets Named

Naming divorce didn't end our marriage. It forced honesty back into it.

Once it was said out loud, we had to confront what we'd been holding in. The resentment. The fatigue. The things we'd stopped asking for because we didn't want to fight again. The lack of time. The lack of space. The lack of real conversation.

We didn't suddenly agree on everything. What changed was that nothing was off-limits anymore.

Uncomfortable topics came back into the room. Hard conversations stopped being delayed indefinitely. We talked about what we needed instead of assuming the other person should just know.

That moment didn't fix everything. It reopened engagement.

Why Exhaustion Is So Dangerous

Burnout doesn't announce itself loudly.

It whispers:

- "It's not worth bringing up."

- "This is just how it is now."

- "We'll deal with it later."

Later often never comes.

Exhaustion convinces people that staying quiet is maturity. That lowering expectations is wisdom. That numbness is stability.

It isn't.

It's a slow exit.

Scripture names this danger clearly.

"Let us consider how we may spur one another on toward love and good deeds."
Hebrews 10:24 (NIV)

Losing connection doesn't always look like betrayal. Sometimes it looks like disengagement.

Exhaustion Is Not Failure, But It Is a Warning

Burnout doesn't mean the marriage is doomed.

It means something essential has been neglected.

Time.

Conversation.

Room for what matters.

Willingness to engage when it's uncomfortable.

Exhaustion is what happens when unity is postponed too long.

It doesn't mean people should give up. It means they need to pay attention.

Key Points

- Most marriages erode quietly, not dramatically

- Numbness often replaces engagement before people leave

- Small fights can expose deeper burnout

- Exhaustion makes silence feel safer than honesty

- Naming what's been avoided can reopen engagement

Questions to Ask Yourself

- Where have I stopped engaging because it feels easier than talking?

- What topics do I avoid because they feel exhausting or risky?

- Where has time together been replaced by efficiency or logistics?

- What needs have I quietly lowered instead of expressing?

- If numbness feels like peace right now, what might I be postponing?

Chapter 8

Listening vs. Fixing

Most people think they know how to listen.

What they usually mean is that they stayed quiet long enough to offer a solution.

That's not listening.

Listening and fixing are not opposites because one is right and the other is wrong. They are opposites because they serve different purposes. Confusing them is one of the fastest ways to pull your partner out of a conversation, even when your intentions are good.

This is where many couples stall after repair has already begun.

Why Fixing Feels Loving

For people who default to fixing, solutions feel like care.

Fixing says:

- I want this to stop hurting.

- I want things to get better.

- I don't want you stuck here.

Fixing creates movement. It reduces uncertainty. It offers direction when things feel overwhelming. To the person doing it, fixing feels responsible, engaged, and loving.

The problem is timing.

When fixing happens before someone feels understood, it doesn't feel helpful. It feels dismissive. Not because the solution is bad, but because the experience hasn't been acknowledged yet.

Fixing answers a question that hasn't been asked.

Why Listening Feels Insufficient

Listening can feel passive to the fixer.

Silence feels like inaction. Questions feel slow. Reflecting back what was heard can feel pointless when the problem seems obvious. Listening can feel like standing still when something clearly needs to be done.

But listening serves a different function.

Listening restores safety.

Listening communicates understanding.

Listening tells the other person they are not alone in what they're carrying.

Without that safety, solutions land as pressure instead of help.

Nonverbal Support Still Counts

Here's something many couples miss.

Support is not only spoken. A lot of support is nonverbal, especially when emotions are high.

Nonverbal support is what keeps the conversation from turning into a courtroom. It communicates, *I'm here*, without turning the moment into a debate.

Nonverbal support can look like:

- staying in the room instead of walking out

- softening your posture instead of squaring up for a fight

- lowering your tone instead of matching volume

- making eye contact instead of rolling your eyes or staring through someone

- nodding to show you're tracking, even if you disagree

- letting silence exist without punishing the other person with it

- pausing before you respond instead of interrupting

This matters because your body can contradict your words. You can say "I'm listening" while your posture says "I'm done." You can say "I care" while your tone says "you're an idiot." You can say "I want to fix this" while your volume says "I want to win."

Nonverbal support doesn't mean you agree. It means you're not making the other person pay a penalty for speaking.

Early in our marriage, I thought listening meant waiting my turn to talk. I would stay quiet, but my body was already arguing. Arms crossed. Jaw tight. Tone sharp when I finally spoke. Cheri could tell immediately that I wasn't actually present, I was preparing a defense. From my perspective, I hadn't interrupted, so I thought I was doing well. From hers, the conversation already felt unsafe before I said a word.

Nothing about that moment required better wording. It required awareness. Until my posture, tone, and pacing matched my intention to listen, the conversation never really started.

Why Fixing Can Feel Like Dismissal

When someone is trying to explain how something felt, fixing often skips the most important step.

It bypasses impact.

The person being listened to isn't asking for an answer yet. They're asking to be known. When fixing comes too soon, it can sound like:

- "This isn't that big of a deal."
- "You shouldn't feel this way."
- "You're overthinking it."

Even when none of that is intended, that's often how it lands.

This is why both people can leave the same conversation feeling unheard at the same time.

Why Listening Alone Isn't Enough Either

Listening is not the final step.

Listening without eventual movement can feel like avoidance. Silence without follow-up can feel like refusal. Being heard but never seeing change creates its own kind of distance.

This is where people who need resolution start to disengage.

Listening restores safety.
Fixing restores direction.

Slowing down to listen is not abandoning responsibility. It is delaying response long enough to make it effective.

The issue is not choosing one. It's sequencing them correctly.

The Order Matters

Most conflict escalation happens because the order gets reversed.

Fixing before listening removes safety.
Listening without ever fixing removes trust.

Healthy conversations tend to follow a simple progression:

- Understanding first

- Response second

This is why statements like:

"This is what I heard, and this is how it made me feel"

matter so much. They slow the conversation down long enough for understanding to happen before solutions enter the room.

Once someone feels heard, fixing no longer feels invasive. It feels collaborative.

Staying in the Conversation

Listening vs fixing is not about personality. It's about awareness.

There are times when listening is what keeps the conversation alive. There are times when fixing is what keeps it moving forward.

The skill is knowing which one is needed *now*.

When people learn to listen long enough to restore safety and fix soon enough to restore direction, conversations stop collapsing under their own weight.

That's how engagement is maintained.

Key Points

- Fixing feels loving to the fixer, not dismissive
- Listening restores safety before solutions can help
- Fixing too soon shuts conversations down

- Listening without response eventually erodes trust

- The problem is usually sequence, not intent

- Understanding first makes fixing collaborative instead of controlling

Questions to Ask Yourself

- When conflict comes up, do I move to fixing before understanding?

- How do I react when listening feels slow or inefficient?

- When have I felt heard but still stuck?

- Where might the order of listening and fixing be reversed in my conversations?

- What would it look like to stay present long enough to understand before responding?

Chapter 9

Words, Timing, and the Weight They Carry

Most conflict is not caused by what is said.
It is caused by when it is said, how it is said, and who is standing nearby when it lands.

People often believe communication problems come from choosing the wrong words. That is rarely the real issue. Words do not land in a vacuum. They land inside context, stress, history, fear, and expectation. The same sentence spoken at a different time or in a different setting can either build safety or quietly tear it apart.

This chapter is not about learning to use positive words instead of negative ones. It is about understanding impact.

When Words Land Wrong

I remember coming home after spending months away for work. I walked into the house and asked a simple question related to something our daughter was learning at the time. It was a phonics concept called hunk and chunk. You combine letters to create a sound. I asked the question casually, thinking it was light and harmless.

It was not.

The timing was wrong. The setting was wrong. Other people were present. The words themselves were not harsh, but the impact was. What I intended as curiosity landed as criticism. What I thought was neutral landed as judgment. The shift happened almost immediately. I felt it before I understood it.

Nothing about the sentence itself explained the reaction. The impact came from everything surrounding it.

Words do not just communicate information. They communicate posture.

Impact Matters More Than Intent

Intent matters. But impact determines what happens next.

Scripture warns against the assumption that urgency justifies speech.

"Those who guard their lips preserve their lives, but those who speak rashly will come to ruin."
Proverbs 13:3 (NIV)

This is not a warning against honesty. It is a warning against haste. Speaking quickly may feel relieving, but relief is not the same as wisdom. Words spoken without restraint often create the very damage they were meant to prevent.

Scripture consistently links wisdom with timing. Wanting to be heard is not the same as being ready to speak. Wanting to fix is not the same as knowing what will heal.

Two people can mean well and still hurt each other deeply. That does not make either one malicious. It means words were spoken without considering timing, capacity, or environment.

When words land badly, the usual responses are predictable.

Fixers speak more.

Processors retreat.

Both responses often make things worse.

The Limits of Communication

This is important to say clearly.

Communication does not solve every conflict.

Some disagreements can be resolved.

Some disagreements can be lived with.

Some disagreements are foundational.

Communication does not erase foundational differences. It reveals them.

- There are things you can agree to resolve.
- There are things you can agree to disagree on and still remain close.
- There are also beliefs that shape identity, direction, and conscience.

Those beliefs do not change because communication improves.

Foundations and Expectations

Do not enter a relationship expecting to change the fundamentals of who your partner is. Inside a healthy relationship, people change together through communication and shared ideals. Fundamentals do not change on demand.

For Cheri and me, shared faith was essential. Without a genuine, shared belief, our marriage would not have worked. Faith was the foundation we built everything else on. We were not identical in how we practiced that faith. I have never believed that faithfulness requires sitting in a church building every Sunday. I believe it requires fellowship with other believers. Cheri goes to church every Sunday and always has.

That difference was real. It was discussed. It was not minimized. It was workable because the foundation itself was shared.

Foundational belief differences do not soften with time. They shape how people raise children, make decisions, and understand meaning and responsibility. If those differences exist, they must be discussed and accepted early. When they are avoided or minimized, they tend to surface later under pressure, and they can end a relationship.

When the Fixer Needs to Pause

Fixers often believe that clarity brings relief. The instinct is to speak quickly, explain thoroughly, and move toward resolution. Sometimes that instinct is exactly what causes harm.

There have been moments where I spoke because I wanted to help. I had the right solution. I had thought it through. I spoke before the other person had the capacity to hear it. The words were not wrong. The timing was.

In those moments, speaking did not create safety. It created distance.

Fixers need to learn that silence can be an act of care. Pausing does not mean disengaging. It means choosing timing over urgency.

When the Processor Needs to Speak

Processors tend to believe that silence creates safety. Sometimes it does. Other times, silence becomes threatening.

There have been moments where Cheri needed reassurance, anchoring, or presence, and my silence did not communicate patience. It communicated absence. I was processing internally while the space between us grew heavier.

Processing is not the problem. Staying silent when presence is needed is.

Processors need to learn that speaking imperfectly can be more stabilizing than staying silent.

Silence is not the same as wisdom. Pausing is not the same as disappearing.

"Everyone should be quick to listen, slow to speak and slow to become angry."
James 1:19 (NIV)

This does not favor silence over speech or patience over action. It calls for discernment. Wisdom is not found in speaking first or waiting longest, but in knowing which moment requires restraint and which requires presence.

Stewarding Conflict Instead of Solving It

Some conflicts cannot be solved. They must be stewarded.

That means learning when to speak and when to wait.

It means learning when to clarify and when to listen.

It means recognizing when the goal is not agreement, but connection.

Communication does not always move a couple toward resolution. Sometimes it determines whether a disagreement becomes corrosive or contained.

Key Points

- Words do not land in isolation. Timing, setting, and audience shape impact.

- Intent does not override impact. Both matter, but impact determines outcome.

- Communication does not resolve every conflict. Some differences are foundational.

- Do not expect to change the fundamentals of your partner. Growth happens together within shared ideals.

- Fixers must learn when to pause. Speaking too soon can create distance.

- Processors must learn when to speak. Silence can feel like abandonment.

- Some conflicts cannot be solved. They must be stewarded.

Reflection Questions

- When have my words landed differently than I intended, and why?

- Do I tend to speak too quickly, or stay silent too long, under stress?

- Are there disagreements in my relationship that are resolvable, livable, or foundational?

- Have foundational beliefs been discussed clearly, or assumed?

- What would it look like to prioritize timing and presence over being right?

Chapter 10

Capacity vs. Pressure: What Gives Way First

When responsibility expands and capacity shrinks, what gives way first is usually the marriage.

That can happen with:

- parenting

- caregiving

- work

- ministry

- crisis

- survival seasons

Pressure usually arrives first. Capacity shrinks in response, emotionally, relationally, and physically.

Parenting just happens to be the most common and relatable entry point.

This chapter is not about doing those things wrong. It's about what gets displaced when life gets heavy and no one is paying attention.

How Displacement Happens

Pressure doesn't arrive politely. It shows up demanding attention. Kids need care. Parents need help. Jobs demand more. Crises don't wait until you're rested or ready.

Capacity does not expand at the same rate.

So something has to give.

What usually gives way is not commitment. It's connection. Time together becomes optional. Conversations get postponed. Emotional energy gets redirected toward whatever feels most urgent.

The marriage doesn't end. It moves to the margins.

Most couples don't notice this happening because it feels responsible. Necessary. Temporary. They tell themselves they'll come back to it when things calm down.

Often, things never fully do.

Parenting as the Pressure Point

Parenting exposes this dynamic faster than almost anything else.

Kids are loud. Needs are constant. Exhaustion is normal. The work feels morally justified. When the marriage starts slipping, it's easy to believe that's just the cost of being good parents.

But what's usually happening is displacement.

The marriage becomes logistical. Conversations revolve around schedules and responsibilities. Time together shrinks. What used to be intentional becomes accidental.

No one chooses this. It happens because pressure is louder than intention.

Survival Mode Shrinks the Marriage

Survival mode is efficient. It is not relational.

When couples are surviving, they stop choosing each other and start getting through the day. That works in the short term. Over time, it creates distance that feels confusing later.

People don't stop loving each other. They stop making room.

This is where exhaustion quietly sets in. Not just physical exhaustion, but relational fatigue. Talking feels like work. Time together feels rare. Important conversations keep getting delayed because there never seems to be enough energy left.

Buying Chairs When Capacity Is Minimal

Buying each other's chairs does not stop when capacity shrinks. It adapts.

There was a season when I was helping care for my stepdad while he was on hospice. Capacity was low. Pressure was constant. There wasn't space for big gestures or ideal connection.

What mattered most during that time was a five-minute coffee break together.

Five minutes. No fixing. No planning. Just choosing to sit together and talk, even briefly.

That small act mattered more than grand intentions. It reminded us that the marriage hadn't been displaced entirely. Even under extreme constraint, we were still choosing each other.

Buying chairs doesn't always look like hobbies, rooms, or space. Sometimes it looks like refusing to let connection disappear completely.

What Gets Lost When Displacement Goes Unnamed

When displacement is left unnamed, couples often don't realize what they've lost until the pressure eases.

Kids get older. Crises pass. Schedules lighten.

And suddenly there's distance where closeness used to be.

This is why some couples feel more disconnected when life slows down instead of closer. The marriage was sidelined for so long that re-engagement feels unfamiliar.

Nothing dramatic happened. No betrayal. No single failure.

Just prolonged neglect.

This Is Not Inevitable

Capacity will shrink again. Pressure will return in new forms.

The question is not whether life will demand more than you have to give. It will.

The question is whether the marriage is intentionally protected when that happens or quietly displaced until later.

Later is rarely as easy as people hope.

Key Points

- When responsibility expands, capacity does not automatically follow

- Something always gives way under pressure

- The marriage is often what gets displaced first

- Parenting is a common trigger, not the root cause

- Survival mode prioritizes efficiency over connection

- Buying chairs adapts when capacity is limited, it does not disappear

Questions to Ask Yourself

- Where has pressure pushed my marriage to the margins?

- What conversations have I postponed because I'm surviving instead of engaging?

- How has time together changed during high-pressure seasons?

- What does buying chairs look like right now with the capacity we actually have?

- If this season lasted longer than expected, what would I want protected?

Even strong communication strains under pressure, and the next place it often breaks isn't in what we feel, but in what we're carrying.

Chapter 11

Work, Money, and Stress

Money problems rarely start with numbers.

They start with fear.

Work stress, financial pressure, and uncertainty don't just strain a marriage practically. They reshape how people think, react, and protect themselves. When money enters the conversation, it often brings anxiety with it. And anxiety changes behavior long before anyone talks about it.

This chapter isn't about budgets or income. It's about what pressure does to people and how that pressure quietly distorts partnership.

How Money Creates Pressure

Money represents more than spending power.

It represents:

- security

- competence

- provision

- control

- future safety

When money feels threatened, people respond instinctively. Some tighten. Some avoid. Some overwork. Some shut down. Some take control. Others disengage.

None of that starts with malice.

It starts with fear.

There was a season when work stress shaped everything in our house.

I was carrying responsibility that felt non-negotiable. The pressure to provide sat on my chest constantly. I didn't talk about it much. I worked more. I stayed mentally occupied instead. I told myself I was being responsible.

What I didn't see was how that pressure changed how I showed up. Conversations shortened. My patience thinned. Decisions felt urgent instead of shared. When Cheri raised concerns, I heard criticism instead of care.

From my side, I felt like I was holding everything together.
From hers, it felt like I was disappearing behind responsibility.

We weren't arguing about money.
We were reacting to fear we hadn't named.

When Work Becomes Survival

Work is often framed as responsibility, and it is. But when work becomes survival, it begins to consume emotional energy that used to belong to the relationship.

Long hours. Mental exhaustion. Constant pressure to perform. Carrying stress home because there's nowhere else to put it.

Over time, the marriage gets what's left.

Not because it matters less, but because everything else feels urgent.

This is how partners start living alongside each other instead of with each other.

Different Stress Responses Create Conflict

Money and work pressure rarely affect both people the same way.

One partner may respond by tightening control. Tracking spending. Limiting risk. Pushing for certainty.

The other may respond by avoiding. Hoping it resolves. Needing space. Trusting things will work out.

Neither response is wrong on its own. The conflict comes when those responses collide without being named.

Control feels suffocating to one.
Avoidance feels irresponsible to the other.

Without understanding the fear underneath, couples fight about behavior instead of addressing what's driving it.

When Money Replaces Trust

Unchecked financial stress often shifts decision-making out of partnership.

One person starts deciding alone. Justifying it as necessary. The other feels excluded, monitored, or infantilized.

Money becomes leverage instead of a shared resource.

This doesn't happen overnight. It happens gradually, under pressure, when fear convinces someone that unity is too risky.

But control is not safety. And financial security built without partnership always costs something relationally.

Work Stress Displaces Connection

Stress narrows focus.

When people are under constant pressure, conversations become transactional. Checklists replace curiosity. Efficiency replaces presence.

Time together feels unproductive. Emotional engagement feels draining. Silence feels easier.

This is not a character flaw. It's a stress response.

But left unaddressed, it erodes connection the same way neglect does.

Buying Chairs Under Financial Pressure

Buying each other's chairs doesn't stop when money is tight. It becomes more intentional.

Under financial pressure, buying chairs often looks like:

- agreeing on priorities instead of acting alone

- making space for rest even when productivity feels urgent

- supporting career changes even when they're scary

- choosing unity over being right

Support doesn't mean agreement. It means willingness.

Choosing partnership when fear is loud is one of the clearest expressions of commitment.

Unity does not mean ignoring reality or avoiding responsibility. It means facing fear and limits together instead of acting alone.

Fear Changes the Rules Unless It's Named

Fear that stays unspoken still operates.

It dictates tone. It drives decisions. It shapes reactions.

Couples who don't name financial fear end up managing symptoms instead of causes. They argue about purchases, hours, and plans without ever addressing the insecurity underneath.

Naming fear doesn't solve it instantly. But it restores partnership.

Pressure does not stay in our schedules or our bank accounts. When capacity shrinks, couples often stop protecting connection and start managing survival instead. That is why intimacy becomes complicated in stressful seasons. Sex can become a demand, a distraction, a substitute, or something avoided entirely. Before we can talk about intimacy with clarity, we have to name the pressure that has been shaping it.

Key Points

- Money problems usually start with fear, not numbers

- Work stress consumes emotional energy before it's noticed

- Different stress responses create conflict if unnamed

- Control often replaces trust under financial pressure

- Financial decisions made without unity erode partnership

- Buying chairs under pressure requires intentional choice

Questions to Ask Yourself

- How do I respond to financial pressure or work stress?

- What fears do I carry that I haven't named out loud?

- Where has stress shifted our relationship into survival mode?

- How do my coping strategies land on my partner?

- What would choosing unity look like when fear is loud?

Chapter 12

Intimacy vs. Sex

Sex and intimacy are not the same thing.

They are related. They influence each other. They can reinforce each other. But they are not interchangeable. Confusing them is one of the most common reasons couples feel disconnected without understanding why.

Many people don't realize this because sex is often the most obvious expression of closeness in a relationship. When it's present, things feel better. When it's gone, people assume intimacy left with it.

That's not usually what happened.

What Intimacy Actually Is

Intimacy is about being known.

It's emotional access. Shared vulnerability. Safety in honesty. The ability to be seen without performing. Intimacy exists when two people feel connected beyond roles, responsibilities, and function.

Intimacy requires:

- trust

- openness

- engagement

- emotional presence

- ongoing attention

None of those require sex.

What Sex Is and Is Not

Sex is physical connection.

It can be intimate. It can also be disconnected, performative, or transactional. Sex does not automatically create intimacy, and intimacy does not automatically result in sex.

This is where many couples get stuck.

When intimacy erodes, sex often becomes the only remaining pathway to connection. For some people, sex is how they feel close. When sex disappears, they don't just miss the physical act. They miss feeling wanted, chosen, and connected.

That doesn't make them weak, immoral, or shallow.

It does mean the relationship needs more than one pathway to connection to survive normal seasons.

When Sex Becomes a Substitute

In relationships where emotional intimacy has been displaced, sex often carries more weight than it was meant to.

Sex starts doing work it cannot sustain:

- reassurance

- validation

- closeness

- stress relief

- emotional regulation

When sex becomes the primary or only form of intimacy, pressure builds quickly. Frequency becomes symbolic. Rejection feels personal. Initiation feels risky. Avoidance feels safer.

This is why arguments about sex are rarely just about sex.

They're about connection.

Why Desire Often Becomes Mismatched

Desire doesn't disappear randomly.

It often follows intimacy.

When emotional closeness fades, desire usually follows. One partner may still seek sex to restore connection. The other may pull away because connection already feels thin.

Both are reacting to the same loss differently.

Without naming the difference between intimacy and sex, couples argue about behavior instead of addressing the gap underneath it.

Intimacy Must Be Rebuilt First

Sex cannot carry what intimacy was meant to hold.

Trying to fix intimacy by focusing only on sex puts pressure in the wrong place. It turns connection into obligation and desire into performance.

When intimacy is rebuilt, sex often follows more naturally. Not because it's demanded, but because connection creates desire instead of replacing it.

This does not mean sex isn't important. It means sex functions best when it is an expression of intimacy, not a replacement for it.

Key Points

- Sex and intimacy are related but not interchangeable

- Intimacy is about being known, not just being close

- Sex can strengthen intimacy but cannot replace it

- Some people experience sex as their primary pathway to intimacy

- That does not make them weak or wrong

- Relationships need multiple forms of connection to survive normal seasons

Questions to Ask Yourself

- How do I personally experience intimacy in this relationship?

- Where have I relied on sex to meet needs intimacy was meant to hold?

- How do I respond when intimacy feels thin or unavailable?

- What other forms of connection have been displaced in our relationship?

- What would rebuilding intimacy look like before focusing on sex?

Chapter 13

Substitution Patterns and Sexual Coping

When intimacy is missing, something usually replaces it.

People do not like emotional voids. When connection feels unavailable, the body and mind look for relief. That relief often comes in the form of distraction, fantasy, withdrawal, or sexual coping.

This is not where most people think the problem starts. It's where it shows up.

What Substitution Actually Is

Substitution is not always conscious.

It's the process of replacing unmet needs with something that offers temporary regulation. That regulation may be physical, emotional, or psychological.

Common substitution patterns include:

- pornography

- sexual fantasy

- emotional withdrawal

- excessive work

- constant distraction

- numbing behaviors

These patterns do not begin with betrayal. They begin with distance.

Pornography as a Coping Pattern

Pornography is one of the most misunderstood substitution patterns.

For some people, pornography is not primarily about sex. It's about:

- stress relief

- emotional regulation

- control

- predictability

- escape

That does not make it harmless. But it does explain why panic and shame do not fix it.

Treating pornography as the problem instead of the symptom often leaves the real issue untouched.

Why Pornography Still Harms Intimacy

Understanding why pornography shows up does not make it harmless.

Pornography trains desire toward consumption instead of connection. It offers arousal without vulnerability, release without engagement, and control without mutuality. Over time, that matters.

Even when it begins as coping, pornography reshapes expectations. It teaches the body to respond without relationship and conditions arousal toward fantasy rather than presence. That erosion does not stay contained.

This is why pornography consistently undermines trust, even when it is hidden carefully. The damage is not only in the secrecy. It's in the way intimacy gets bypassed instead of rebuilt.

Condemning pornography is not about condemning the person using it. It's about being honest about what the pattern does to a relationship. Something can be understandable and still destructive. Understanding a pattern does not excuse coercion, secrecy, or behavior that removes choice or safety from the other person.

Naming that truth is not cruelty. It's clarity.

Why Secrecy Makes It Worse

Secrecy intensifies substitution.

When something becomes hidden, it gains power. Shame grows. Distance increases. Trust erodes quietly.

Secrecy does not exist because someone wants to betray their partner. It exists because they don't know how to talk about what's missing without causing harm or conflict.

That doesn't excuse secrecy. It explains why it persists.

Avoidance Is Also a Sexual Pattern

Not all sexual coping looks like pursuit.

Avoidance is also a pattern.

Some people withdraw sexually when intimacy feels unsafe. They shut down desire, minimize needs, or convince themselves it doesn't matter.

This can look like:

- loss of interest

- constant fatigue

- emotional numbness

- discomfort with vulnerability

Avoidance protects the self when connection feels risky.

Why Panic Fails

Panic treats substitution as a moral emergency.

But panic:

- increases secrecy

- reinforces shame

- escalates control

- avoids the deeper conversation

Fear-driven responses focus on stopping behavior instead of understanding why it started.

That rarely works.

What Actually Helps

Substitution patterns weaken when intimacy strengthens.

That does not mean instant trust or immediate change. It means addressing the gap instead of policing the symptom.

Helpful responses include:

- naming distance honestly

- restoring emotional safety

- rebuilding non-sexual intimacy

- addressing pressure and fear

- inviting accountability without surveillance

This is slower work. It's also more durable.

Scripture and Desire

Scripture does not ignore desire. It places it in context.

"Flee from sexual immorality."
1 Corinthians 6:18 (NIV)

"Above all else, guard your heart, for everything you do flows from it."
Proverbs 4:23 (NIV)

That instruction is not about fear. It's about wisdom. Desire without connection eventually turns inward and destructive.

Avoidance alone is not enough. Redirection matters.

Key Points

- Substitution patterns emerge when intimacy is missing

- Pornography is often a coping mechanism, not the root problem

- Secrecy increases the power of substitution

- Avoidance is also a sexual coping pattern

- Panic and shame make patterns stronger, not weaker

- Addressing the gap matters more than policing behavior

Questions to Ask Yourself

- What do I reach for when connection feels unavailable?

- Where have I avoided conversations about intimacy or distance?

- What fears keep me from naming what I need?

- How do my coping patterns affect trust?

- What would addressing the gap look like instead of managing symptoms?

Where This Leaves Us

Substitution patterns tell the truth about distance long before people are ready to hear it.

They are signals. Not sentences.

In the next chapter, we'll talk about rebuilding trust and connection after distance, not by pretending patterns never existed, but by learning how to stay present through repair.

Chapter 14

Habits That Shape a Marriage

Most marriages don't change because of a single decision.

They change because of repetition.

What you do consistently matters more than what you promise occasionally. Habits form the environment your marriage lives in. Over time, they either make connection easier or make distance automatic.

This chapter is about the small, repeated choices that quietly shape a relationship.

Habits Are Neutral Until They Aren't

Habits are not inherently good or bad.

They are simply patterns repeated often enough to feel normal. The danger is not in having habits. The danger is in not noticing what they are shaping.

Many couples don't choose habits intentionally. They fall into them. Over time, those habits begin to run the relationship without being questioned.

Distance rarely arrives dramatically. It settles in gradually through unexamined routines.

What You Practice Grows

Every marriage practices something.

Some practice avoidance.

Some practice sarcasm.

Some practice efficiency.

Some practice silence.

Some practice conflict.

Others practice checking in.

They practice honesty.

They practice repair.

They practice presence.

None of these are accidental.

What you practice grows stronger. What you neglect weakens.

Habits Either Reduce or Increase Friction

Healthy habits reduce friction. They make it easier to reconnect after stress. They lower the emotional cost of honesty. They shorten recovery time after conflict.

Unhealthy habits increase friction. They make conversations feel heavy. They train people to brace themselves. They make repair feel risky or exhausting.

This is why two couples can face similar pressure and end up in very different places. The difference is often habitual, not circumstantial.

Small Habits Carry Moral Weight

Not because they are dramatic, but because they are repeated.

Tone.

Timing.

Responsiveness.

Follow-through.

These communicate value long before big conversations ever happen.

Ignoring small habits while hoping for large change rarely works.

Habits and Desire

Habits shape desire more than intention alone does.

When connection is practiced daily, desire often follows. When distance is practiced daily, desire fades without anyone deciding to withdraw.

This is why waiting for motivation before changing behavior is usually backward. Behavior often leads motivation, not the other way around.

Building Habits That Support Staying

Healthy habits do not require perfection.

They require consistency.

Helpful habits often include:

- checking in before problems escalate

- repairing quickly after missteps

- naming stress instead of acting it out

- making room for connection even briefly

- revisiting conversations instead of abandoning them

None of these are impressive. All of them are effective.

Habits Expose Priorities

What you make time for reveals what you value.

That doesn't mean you don't care. It means something else is getting practiced more often.

Habits tell the truth about priorities faster than words ever will.

Scripture and Practice

Scripture connects practice and formation clearly.

"Do not merely listen to the word, and so deceive yourselves. Do what it says."
James 1:22 (NIV)

Transformation follows obedience, not intention.

Key Points

- Marriages change through repetition, not declarations

- Habits shape the emotional environment of a relationship

- What is practiced grows stronger over time

- Small behaviors carry long-term weight

- Desire often follows behavior, not intention

- Habits reveal priorities more honestly than words

Questions to Ask Yourself

- What habits currently define our relationship?

- Which habits reduce friction and which increase it?

- Where do my daily behaviors contradict my stated values?

- What small habit could make connection easier this week?

- What would practicing repair look like consistently?

Looking Ahead

Habits shape daily life, but staying well ultimately depends on whether you're willing to choose again when progress feels slow and change feels unfinished.

Chapter 15

The Long View

Most marriages don't fall apart in a single moment.

They fade over time, through discouragement, impatience, and the quiet belief that effort shouldn't have to last this long. People don't usually leave because nothing worked. They leave because the work stopped feeling worth it.

This chapter is about staying when progress is slow. When change feels boring. When the emotional payoff doesn't arrive on schedule.

This is the long view.

Staying Is Not a Feeling

Feelings change quickly. Seasons last longer.

If staying were based on how connected you feel on a given day, no marriage would survive real life. The work of staying is rarely dramatic. It is often quiet, repetitive, and unnoticed.

Staying looks like:

- continuing conversations that don't resolve immediately

- practicing habits that don't feel rewarding yet

- choosing repair even when resentment resurfaces

- re-engaging after disappointment

This is not weakness. It is endurance.

Progress Is Often Invisible While It's Happening

One of the hardest parts of change is that it rarely feels like change in the moment.

You don't notice progress while you're still tired. While old patterns still show up. While mistakes still happen. While arguments still occur.

Progress is usually seen in hindsight.

The danger is assuming nothing is happening just because things aren't perfect yet.

Relapse Does Not Mean Failure

Old patterns return under stress. That's normal.

Relapse does not mean the work didn't matter. It means pressure revealed what still needs attention. The mistake couples make is treating relapse as proof that staying isn't working.

What matters is not whether old behaviors show up again. What matters is how quickly they're recognized, addressed, and repaired.

That's growth.

The Temptation to Stop Trying

There is a moment many couples reach where they stop pushing forward and simply manage coexistence.

They stop having hard conversations.

They stop expecting growth.

They stop believing change is possible.

This moment rarely feels dramatic. It feels practical.

But it's often where marriages quietly stall.

Staying well requires resisting the urge to settle into emotional minimalism.

Becoming, Not Fixing

Early in marriage, the question is often: *How do we fix this?*

Over time, the better question becomes: *Who are we becoming together?*

Fixing focuses on problems. Becoming focuses on direction.

The long view is not about eliminating conflict. It's about shaping the kind of relationship you are building through how you respond to it.

Choosing Again

Staying is not a one-time decision.

It's a series of choices made in ordinary moments. Choosing to listen again. Choosing to repair again. Choosing to engage instead of withdraw. Choosing to make room even when capacity is low.

These choices don't always feel heroic. They feel repetitive.

That repetition is the point.

Scripture and Endurance

Scripture speaks often about perseverance, not because it is easy, but because it is necessary.

> *"Let us not become weary in doing good, for at the proper time we will reap a harvest if we do not give up."*
> **Galatians 6:9 (NIV)**

The harvest doesn't arrive on demand. It comes to those who keep showing up.

Staying Well

Staying well does not mean staying perfectly.

It means staying engaged. Staying honest. Staying willing. Staying open to growth even when the pace feels slow.

The long view is not about enduring misery. It's about committing to the kind of marriage that is built deliberately, over time, through intention rather than impulse.

This is not a call to stay in harm or abuse. Those situations require protection and help. This is a call to recognize the difference between discomfort and destruction, between slow growth and harm.

Final Thoughts

Staying is harder than running because it requires presence.

Presence through boredom.

Presence through frustration.

Presence through seasons where nothing feels resolved yet.

But staying is also how something deeper is built.

Not quickly.

Not easily.

But honestly.

Key Points

- Staying is a repeated choice, not a single decision

- Progress often feels invisible while it's happening

- Relapse does not mean failure

- Discouragement is a greater threat than conflict

- The long view shifts focus from fixing to becoming

Questions to Ask Yourself

- Where have I mistaken slow progress for no progress?

- What habits am I tempted to abandon because they feel unrewarding?

- How do I respond when old patterns resurface?

- Who are we becoming together through this season?

- What does choosing again look like right now?

Closing

Learning how to stay is not about holding on at all costs. It's about staying present long enough for something lasting to form.

That is the work.

A Prayer for Learning to Stay

God,

We come to You without a plan to fix everything.
We come aware that what we don't see in ourselves often
costs the most in our marriages.

Give us the courage to notice our own patterns before we
explain someone else's.
Slow us down enough to hear not just words, but fear,
exhaustion, and hope beneath them.

Teach us to recognize when we are protecting ourselves
instead of protecting the relationship.
When we are fixing instead of listening.
When we are controlling instead of trusting.
When staying feels costly and leaving feels easier to
explain.

Give us eyes to see our part without drowning in shame.
Give us language for what we feel before it turns into
distance or silence.
Help us tell the truth gently, and hear the truth without
defensiveness.

Where our communication has become unsafe, bring
safety back first.
And where there is harm, intimidation, or abuse,
give us the courage to tell the truth about that as well.

Help us understand that staying does not mean enduring harm,
and faithfulness does not require silence in the face of abuse.
Give wisdom to know when help is needed beyond ourselves,
and courage to seek it without guilt or fear.

Remind us that staying is not something we perform perfectly,
but something we practice imperfectly, together, over time.

When we are tired, teach us rest instead of withdrawal.
When we are afraid, teach us curiosity instead of control.
When we don't know what to say, teach us how to listen.

Help us become more aware of ourselves so that we can be more present with each other.
Help us choose unity over winning, honesty over comfort, and love over fear.

We place our marriages, our conversations, and our unfinished places in Your care.
Teach us how to stay and, when necessary, how to seek safety and help,
one honest moment at a time.

Amen.

If One Place Feels Close Right Now

You do not need to read everything at once.

Often, one area feels closer or heavier than the others. If that is true for you, it may help to begin with Scripture that gives language to that place before trying to resolve it.

If communication feels tense, defensive, or unsafe, these chapters helped us slow down and listen more carefully:
Proverbs 18
James 1
Ephesians 4

If one of you feels unheard while the other feels responsible to fix everything, these chapters helped us recognize posture before solutions:
Romans 12
Philippians 2
Proverbs 20

If resentment or control has crept in quietly, these chapters helped us name what was being carried without being spoken:
Matthew 20
Luke 22
Galatians 5

If intimacy has become tangled with avoidance, pressure, or coping, these chapters helped us separate closeness from performance and fear:
1 Corinthians 13
Song of Songs 2
1 Thessalonians 4

If you are exhausted and afraid that staying means losing yourself, these chapters helped us understand rest, limits, and endurance:
Matthew 11
Psalm 62
Galatians 6

You do not have to read all of these. One chapter may be enough for now. Sometimes the most faithful step is not understanding everything, but letting yourself be named honestly in one place.

Staying is learned slowly. Clarity often comes before change.

A Final Word

If you have reached the end of this book, you have already done something difficult. You stayed present long enough to look honestly at yourself, your patterns, and your relationships. That matters more than doing everything right.

You do not need to carry every idea from these pages forward at once. Staying is not proven by effort, but by attention. Sometimes the most faithful next step is simply noticing what feels different than it did before.

This book was written as a companion to *Stop Running*, which tells the story that came before this one. If *Learning How to Stay* speaks to what it takes to remain, *Stop Running* speaks to the places that taught us to leave. Some readers begin there. Others come back to it later. There is no order you have to follow.

For those who find it helpful to walk alongside others asking similar questions, we quietly host a space for shared reflection and conversation. You are welcome if and when that feels useful.

More than anything, we hope this book helped you feel less alone in the work of staying. You are not behind. You are not failing. You are learning, slowly, what it means to remain present and honest in love.

That is enough for today.

www.ingramcontent.com/pod-product-compliance
Lightning Source LLC
Chambersburg PA
CBHW062101270326
41931CB00013B/3167